THE SIX
ESSENTIALS
OF RAPIDLY
GROWING
NONPROFITS

DOUGLAS K. SHAW

TABLE OF CONTENTS

INTRODUCTION

In my more than 40 years of raising money for organizations, I've had the privilege of serving more than 300 nonprofits. When I first began my journey on this road reaching out into the great philanthropic unknown, I would never have guessed that one day I would be writing the words you've just read!

I was almost 30 years old when I took my first steps on this path. I had a head full of hair, a heart full of hope, and millions of questions about fundraising. Like most fundraisers, I had no formal training for the trail ahead of me. But one thing I did have was a deep passion to see goodness, justice, and positive belief advanced in a world filled with people who needed faith and hope.

Wrapped up in my passion was also a propelling desire to have a useful role in making a difference in our world. Simply put, I craved knowledge and gifts that would allow me to succeed, to have a clear sense of calling, and to know I was doing exactly what I believed God wanted me to be doing. But at age 30, I had very little assurance of any of this.

It's only by looking back in time that I can now see how I was being molded into what I am today, a 70-year-old veteran fundraiser who has traveled great distances and seen many wonders along the way.

But this book isn't about me. It's about you and your organization. What follows has been written to help you get some of your own questions answered as you take yet another step in *your* journey. I offer it to you as a fellow traveler who has seen a little of what lies just around the bend. May it provide you with a greater sense of direction as you navigate the paths of a life of service.

RAPIDLY GROWING NONPROFITS

Every organization has a start date. At some point in earthbound time, the God of eternity breathes life into a vision, a desire, a hope, or maybe just a dream. What an amazing creation moment!

For some organizations, it begins with an individual. For others, it occurs when several like-minded people find each other and dare to express their hearts' desires with kindred spirits.

Throughout the years, I've had the privilege of hearing several of these creation stories, and it seems that no two are exactly alike. In fact, all of creation itself testifies to God's preference for diversity!

Not only are organizational beginnings diverse, but most nonprofit leaders I know are quick to point out that their organization is "unique," an idea I readily accept. But I have also observed some shared attributes among organizations, especially those growing exponentially.

On the occasions when I have communicated these shared attributes, it has been met with great interest. It's my hope that these thoughts will be of service to you.

Over the decades, I've had the privilege of observing the growth of many different kinds of nonprofit organizations. Most grow at a fairly steady pace, others have found themselves in decline, and yet others, for several reasons, are rapidly growing organizations. Here is a list of what I have observed to be the essential qualities of rapidly growing organizations:

1. Dynamic Leadership
2. Clear Vision Articulated by the Leadership
3. A Mission Donors Can Relate to and Support
4. Followers Who Support the Vision, Mission, and Leader
5. Resources That Can Be Allocated for Growth
6. The Will to Employ Those Available Resources

Whenever I've shared this list with people in nonprofits, they begin counting off, on their fingers, the number of these attributes they believe their own organization has in place. It usually plays out like this: "Yes, yes, maybe, no, no, nope. I think we might have three of these." You may want to see how many of these essential attributes your organization has.

This book is for the "C-Suite." You know, the people who have titles beginning with the letter "C": CEOs, COOs, CFOs, and CDOs (chief development officers). But it's also for those who have roles that begin with "B" or "T," board members or trustees, whichever designation your organization chooses to use. Let's not stop there, though, because left on their own, they can accomplish very little. I don't say this to diminish the C-Suite. Rather, I'm merely pointing out that there's another "C," i.e., colleagues or followers, if you will. If you work in a nonprofit organization, this book is written with you in mind as well. I believe you'll see the truth and value of this statement as we move along.

ESSENTIAL #1
DYNAMIC LEADERSHIP

As you know, there is an entire industry built around leadership and leadership principles. So, in this chapter, I'm going to limit my comments strictly to my own observations of highly effective leaders of rapidly growing organizations in the nonprofit charity space.

My conversations with leaders within this community lead me to believe you may be interested in looking at your own leadership in comparison to other leaders of rapidly growing organizations. For this reason, you're not reading yet another book on "How to Become a More Effective Leader." That's already been done, time and again, by persons much more qualified than I. In this chapter, what follows are my observations of the *essential attributes* of a dynamic leader in a rapidly growing nonprofit organization.

The first attribute I've seen in leaders of rapidly growing organizations is that they are clearly in the right chair. When observed in action, few can doubt it. These leaders exude positivity about accomplishing their mission. You won't usually find them spending an inordinate amount of time looking in the mirror, either at themselves, with admiration, or in the rearview mirror, mourning the mistakes of the past. They're not thinking about themselves much at all; there's simply too much to accomplish!

This dynamic leader has a very strong work ethic. He fully realizes the amount of time and energy required to move an organization in the right direction. He knows full well the weight of the responsibility that has been accepted by taking on the mantle of leadership. He knows that being the leader does not mean arrival at the proverbial "top," but rather, understands leadership to be what the late Max DePree described as "a posture of indebtedness." DePree spent many pages in his book

Leadership Is an Art probing the concept of the *indebtedness* of leaders, by delineating what a leader owes to those following him. I highly recommend this book, and all of the writings of Max DePree, to anyone interested in the concept of the indebtedness of leadership.

In addition to the broader attributes of inspired leaders, there is a firm grasp of reality in the leader of a rapidly growing organization. Sometimes it is best evidenced in the face of opposition. As the Massachusetts lawyer John Adams declared while defending the British soldiers of the famed Boston Massacre, "Facts are stubborn things!" As you may remember, he persuaded a Boston jury to acquit the crowd-provoked soldiers of the Crown.

For the inspired leader, identifying and articulating reality are not limited simply to the grand scope of things. Forward thinking and hard-driving focus are not substitutes for the realities of the day. Payroll must still be met. Budgets must be balanced. Momentum and reach cannot be allowed to cloud or overlook daily decisions. But understanding reality is not the sole province of this leader. Every person in the organization must understand and embrace the future in light of the current surroundings, but the burden of identifying and communicating reality is clearly a primary responsibility of their leader.

Another confirmation that a leader of a rapidly growing nonprofit is in the right chair is the ability of this person to make decisions in a timely manner. But far more important than the *ability* to make decisions is the leader's *capability* to see the near- and far-reaching implications of a decision. For example, some questions that arise in the process of decision-making might include:

- Do I have the authority to make this decision? Or does this decision require board approval?
- Am I the appropriate person to make this decision? Is there someone else within the organization who should be making this

decision as part of her/his own authority and responsibility?

- <u>What is the "regret level"</u>? If this decision is made, will I regret having made it in the future? Will I regret NOT making this decision in the future?

- <u>Is this a precedent-setting decision</u>? If so, am I willing to live with the legacy of this decision?

- <u>What are the political implications of making this decision</u>? Are there issues that could arise beyond the obvious and immediate? Will they come from inside the organization? Will there be public resistance or outcry?

- <u>Do I need input</u> in making this decision? Is there more information required to make a solid decision? What level of buy-in is needed within the executive team? Broader leadership team? Staff?

- <u>How do I communicate</u> that this decision has been made? What channels do I use? To whom?

As I've observed, one cannot be a leader without encountering a significant number of questions that require thoughtful answers while building a rapidly growing organization.

Nor can dynamic leadership occur without encountering conflict among the people being led, a constituency being served, or a public that both benefits from and financially supports the organization. An effective leader is able to live in a world of conflicting ideas, principles, behaviors, and actions. A leader who is in the right chair knows this responsibility well and will not shrink from it, nor will a leader of this caliber foment conflict needlessly.

You and I have likely been in positions where our leaders fell far short in the area of conflict management. In most of these situations I've seen, one of two malfunctions occurs, much to the detriment of the organization's culture and viability.

The first and most common malfunction I've experienced, both as an employee and later as a consultant, is *conflict avoidance*. Let's face it, who wants to wade into the middle of two people or factions who are in heated disagreement with each other? To someone who is experiencing conflict avoidance, it may feel a bit like coming between a mother bear and her cubs! No one that I can think of looks forward to sorting out significant conflict, but an inspired leader knows it must be done.

Unfortunately, many gifted leaders just can't bring themselves to say difficult things to their followers. This is the case with many of the leaders I have known. The resulting damage to their organization is immense. Their employees are left to find their own solutions, which are often at odds with each other and therefore not in the best interest of the organization or its corporate culture. This lack of willingness or ability to bring about conflict resolution often leads to the decision of valuable followers to leave the organization and seek out a more functional corporate culture where they can feel supported. Everyone loses in this scenario.

The heartbreak of this situation is that, for the leader, this is an entirely self-inflicted wound. For a leader to see or experience conflict within the organization she is leading and do nothing about it erodes her leadership and, over time, erodes the feeling of trust in her followers. But this doesn't have to be!

The good news is, the leader who is unwilling or unable to negotiate his way through conflict can, if he is willing to recognize this trait in himself, resolve issues like this when they arise. And the beauty of it all is, the solution is quite easy . . . for him! Junior high and high school principals figured it out a long time ago! Let the vice principal handle conflicts when they happen! A competent COO can be delegated this responsibility, leaving the CEO to be "the good cop," if you will.

The second malfunction I've observed is the *inability to delegate*. It is my observation that this malfunction is much more difficult to overcome than conflict avoidance. It's one thing for a leader to admit to himself that there are certain things he is not good at (e.g., resolving conflicts). It's quite another to have a leader admit that he has difficulty delegating. This malfunction carries a serious stigma that is closely akin to . . . say, something like drinking too much! Who wants to own up to that? Haven't we all been taught that to be an effective leader, you have to know how to delegate?

The truth is, this malfunction in a leader can be a career killer, or at best a career limiter. In my early years as a leader, this was one of my greatest fears; that I would become one of those leaders whom people talked about, saying things like, "He's a great guy, but he just can't delegate." I shuddered at the thought! This fear made me take self-inventory on a regular basis.

Fortunately, I was given the opportunity to sit under some very gifted leaders who were able to articulate the essentials of leadership. I remember well the day I heard one of these respected mentors say, "You simply cannot do everything! A leader is a person who gets things done through other people." I really liked hearing this, but the real jewel in this mentoring session was when this mentor said, "You will have people who report to you who cannot do things as well as you do. This will be very hard for you to watch. *You will need to allow them to do things only 80 percent as well as you would do them!*" These words jumped out at me. They both frightened me and freed me! My fright came when I thought about the 20 percent of the work that might not be done correctly, but my freedom came in realizing that somebody was taking the same risk in allowing me to become a leader. I came to think of this insightful leadership principle as "the grace factor." Just as I was being granted the grace of growing into my job, I needed to allow those reporting to me this same grace.

There is another significant benefit to learning how to delegate. This benefit has more to do with the quantity of work I was leaving undone. If I really believed that I could not do everything, then to have one of my reports pick up 80 percent of the 100 percent that I could not do (since I couldn't do everything), delegation was becoming a very inspiring and motivating point of awareness. Delegation was not only allowing my reports to grow and flourish, it was getting more done than I could do myself! It's my hope that my mentor's words can provide you with the same freedom that I have had the joy to experience.

Inspired leaders know the advantage of asking the right questions, the courage of wading into the fray when conflict arises, and the necessity of delegating to their followers.

Another indicator that this leader is in the right chair is his intelligence. This trait, which will be evident to all, is shown largely because of his unending willingness to *ask questions*, as opposed to *making pronouncements*. The questions themselves will reveal the leader's high level of intelligence stemming from his insatiable curiosity.

Further proof that this leader is in the right role is measured by her continual pursuit of excellence in all she thinks, does, and requires. To her, the drive for excellence comes as naturally as breathing. She knows there is a significant difference between *excellence* and *perfection*. Excellence is achievable, whereas perfection is not. She is leading imperfect people, which is all there are, but she knows they can be led to the path of excellence.

It is this leader's ability to identify, articulate, and adhere to the organization's *core values* that gives him the credibility to call others to this same standard of excellence. Once identified and articulated, the adherence to the organization's core values becomes the position description of the leader in executing the vision and mission entrusted to him.

Vigilance of this sacred trust is the province of the leader of a rapidly growing nonprofit. It is the extent to which the leader can convince her followers to embrace this practice of vigilance in adhering to the core values that will determine the long-term viability of the organization.

A leader who is in the right chair communicates with pristine clarity all that the vision, mission, and core values embody. These are likely some of the most critical aspects of this leader's role.

A second major attribute I have witnessed in leaders of rapidly growing organizations is an innate ability to inspire others. It's impossible to be in the presence of this leader without being stirred by the total commitment to his vision, the absolute belief that the mission driving him can and will be accomplished, and his intensity of purpose and desire for speed. Inspiration emanates from every breath, word, and pore. This somewhat fanatical presence likely carries with it a certain amount of intimidation. Let me be quick to explain: Intimidation is not a goal of this leader; it is, in my observation, most often an undesired outcome.

I had the privilege of working with a well-known author, professor, and radio personality. He is one of the most inspiring leaders I've had the privilege to serve over the years. His ability to think, write, and speak in an extremely unique style allowed him to connect with his readers, students, and listeners as few can.

On one occasion, I had the opportunity to join him for dinner on the night he had just completed writing a very important and lengthy novel. I remember asking him how it felt to begin this significant work. He replied, "It's like building a bridge, but you don't know where it will touch down on the other end." Since by this time he had authored more than 25 books, I figured he knew what he was talking about. I sat there next to him, feeling a little intimidated by his accomplishments. But this was nothing compared to the next day . . .

It was an hour before this great man was to speak to an audience of about 500 people. He had sequestered himself inside the sanctuary of the church where he was to speak. I remember reaching for the door to the sanctuary when his agent quickly stopped me. Her eyes grew wide, and she whispered, "Whatever you do, don't go in there!" "What's he doing?" I whispered back. "He's pacing!" she replied. "It's what he always does before he speaks! If you want to see what I mean, come with me." She took me through a side door that led to the pulpit. She stopped just short of entering and instructed, "Just stick your head in quickly, look at him, and then come back without him seeing you." Not only was I totally fascinated by what I might see, but I was also very intimidated and nervous. I was going to spy on this man!

Quietly opening the door, I walked softly through the rear entrance to the pulpit. Peeking ever so slightly around the edge of what felt like a secret passage, I could see him. He was pacing way up in the balcony, talking and gesturing to himself. His energy reminded me of a panther about to pounce. I exited quickly, hoping that I had not been discovered. Upon emerging from the back door, his agent said to me, "This is how he prepares. He paces while he organizes his thoughts. You see, he doesn't use notes."

When he spoke that afternoon, I was even more impressed with this great leader. His message was eloquent and relevant, and his style was uniquely his. The panther had indeed pounced! He was challenging this august body of leaders to think differently. His intensity captivated us all. Over the years, as I came to know this man a little better, I realized that he had no intention of being intimidating. But he had every intention of communicating the truth as he experienced it in ways that were highly creative and with great energy! He is truly an inspired leader.

For a leader of this kind, this energy is completely contagious and extends in all directions. The board of trustees is highly impacted by this type of leader. All passivity is driven from the room when she enters the boardroom. There is no place to hide. Policy decisions become more far-reaching and perhaps more uncomfortable, yet carry an excitement not commonly experienced. The leader's energy infuses the board, and their hearts are lifted to a place of higher calling and greater wisdom, which they in turn impart to the inspired leader. This is when the truth of, "As iron sharpens iron, so one person sharpens another" (Proverbs 27:17, NIV) becomes the example to everyone within the rapidly growing nonprofit.

A truly inspired leader will be a strong and frequent communicator to the trustees, flooding them with the knowledge of the far-reaching impact of their decisions. As positive impact increases, the true will of this critical body will be tested as never before. The inspired leader is fully cognizant that he serves at the pleasure of this group and as the ambassador to the trustees on behalf of his staff. The policies emanating from the board become fuel he needs to provide clarity and direction to the staff of this organization.

When observing the staff of a rapidly growing organization, there is magic. Everyone is aware that they are part of something special. Energy and ideas bubble up amongst the staff as well as their leadership. The excitement of achieving their mission provides the impetus to push through their feelings of the unintended intimidation radiating from their leader. They are certain of the power of any good idea that will propel their mission forward. This freedom of ideation expands exponentially within the organization, and the world is changed.

An inspired leader uses this force for good in propelling the mission forward. It is often the ideas of the staff that provide the inspired leader's agenda for the trustees.

With this dynamic cycle of shared purpose and freedom of expression, communication to the public crackles with energy. Donors catch this sense of being a part of history and want to contribute. Donations increase rapidly to supply the ever-expanding vision of the inspired leader.

The positive impact of accomplishing the mission carries the trustees, inspired leader, staff, and donors to a place of tapping into divine power where "thinking inside the box" has no place. Obstacles give birth to a frantic search for resolution. Walls that pop up are scaled, tunneled under, bypassed, and left behind but not forgotten.

An inspired leader helps her organization to remember and respect the traditions that drew their organization into existence. The vision, sacrifice, bravery, and entrepreneurial spirit of those who came before, those who brought them to this point in time, are honored but not worshipped. The inspired leader helps all around her to determine which traditions to keep and which to release.

The rapidly growing organization becomes a culture that studies, values, and embraces innovation in the pursuit of accomplishing its mission. And it is here that the inspired leader exhibits his understanding of his vision for the organization and is willing to exchange it for emerging ideas that reshape the organization's vision and, sometimes, even the mission. The inspired leader knows that things change. Yes, sometimes, on rare occasions, it may involve changing the mission.

When it does, it's done with a sense of divine direction, prayer, great care, and much counsel, both within the organization and from trusted outside counsel. It must ALWAYS involve extensive board discussion and, ultimately, its approval.

It is the inspired leader's emotional maturity that stabilizes and creates a sense of well-being for those who choose to follow him. He experiences, expresses, and shares the full spectrum of his emotions. His understanding of the impact of his emotional vulnerabilities creates confidence in his followers. He is fully human, yet he understands the consequences of everything he says and does. For this reason, he realizes the benefits of being in control of his emotions. This is not meant to imply a stoic persona. Inspired leaders laugh, cry, and rejoice too. It simply means he understands and attempts to practice the *benefits* of maintaining self-control and discerning that for him to lose control would be unproductive or harmful.

A person leads a rapidly growing nonprofit with obvious intelligence. Even though she has a higher-than-average IQ, she knows her limits and compensates for them with her keen eye for talent embodied in trusted long-term relationships within her circle of leader-confidants (leadership team). She is keenly aware that it is this prized group who are able to absorb her energy, contribute their own, and then radiate it to all who choose to be involved in their beloved enterprise. She knows her leader-confidants are there to provide their own energy, personalities, and expertise not only to their own followers, but also to their leader when she finds her own strengths inadequate or diminishing.

This highly valued leader also knows his time of frontline leadership will, at some point, inevitably come to an end. Embracing this reality is the true indicator of his ability to lead. The task of initiating a succession plan falls squarely upon him. At first, he must face it alone. In this moment, the loneliness can appear overwhelming, yet he knows the perils of neglecting this supremely important transition. Many excellent leaders have allowed their passion for their mission to push off any ideas of life after them. The leader of a rapidly growing nonprofit knows in his heart of hearts that to fail in the mission-critical task of succession planning may well jeopardize the future of everything that has been done thus far.

When an organization's leader is highly functioning, only she knows when to begin the risk of expressing the need for her succession and the succession of her leader-confidants. She knows the challenges of initiating discussions of this transition. Trustees know how difficult it will be to find a leader like the one currently serving and may desire to slow or derail the process. Leader-confidants will each respond to thoughts of succession in their own way. Some may quickly adapt, while others may find it threatening to discuss their own replacements. Staff most often experience leadership change as unsettling, especially concerning how this change may impact their own lives. Major donors who have developed relationships with this leader can become unsettled, and the average supporter can also be shaken when a longtime, beloved leader begins stepping away. Knowing this, the inspired leader will exercise great wisdom in the planned process of information sharing about this next great step in leadership.

Once the decision is made to begin the succession process, the inspired leader moves into a posture of hopeful preparation. There is pleasure in identifying and mentoring emerging leaders and evaluating existing leaders' potential for moving the organization into the future.

Trustees are critical allies in this process. Any final decisions regarding the CEO role and other roles as specified in any solid governance policy will need to apply. The inspired leader also knows that not all trustees are suitable confidants in succession planning.

He is keenly aware that wherever there is power and position, there are politics that can resist the momentum that has been carefully crafted. Yet he knows he does not have the final say. This critical decision is the province of the board.

NOTES:

NOTES:

ESSENTIAL #2
CLEAR VISION ARTICULATED BY THE LEADERSHIP

"Every vision is a joke until the first man accomplishes it; once realized, it becomes commonplace."
—*Robert Goddard, the founding father of rocket engineering*

Today, I'm a CEO of my own company. But this has only been the case for 25 of my 67 years. Vision, for me, had a very literal meaning when I was 12 years old and in seventh grade. My grades were not particularly good in junior high. I was one of those kids who liked to sit in the back of the classroom, where I found it very easy to become interested in what was going on outside the window, what other kids around me were doing, and almost anything other than what was happening in the front of the classroom.

One day, my teacher called me to the front of the class. "Doug, I'd like for you to sit here," she said, pointing to a desk in the front row. The class chuckled, because nobody wanted to sit in the front row, except for that irritating guy who knew the answer to every question.

Motioning for me to take my new seat, the teacher resumed her instruction. As she turned to the chalkboard and began writing, she glanced back at me to make certain that I was now paying attention. What she saw was me squinting, trying to make out what she was writing on the board. She did something that I am grateful for to this day. She asked, "Doug, can you see what I'm writing?" I replied quietly, "No, not really." She instructed me to stand up and move my desk closer to the blackboard and then take my seat. "Can you see now?" she asked. Sheepishly I replied, "No, not really." Again, she said, "Doug, will you move your desk closer to the board until you CAN see what I'm writing?" I did as I was instructed. I was now in my own personal front row . . . two feet from the blackboard!

When the bell rang, my teacher asked me to remain after class. I knew I must be in REALLY BIG TROUBLE. She sat at her desk writing something while I just stood there in front of her. When she was done, she folded her note in half and handed it to me while saying, "Give this note to your parents when you get home." I took it and scrambled out the door mumbling something like "thank you." Running to my locker, I spun the combination lock quickly, opened the door, and used it as a shield to read what she had written . . .

Mr. and Mrs. Shaw,

I'm writing to ask that you take Doug to an eye doctor. He is having trouble reading what I write on the blackboard. I believe it is affecting his ability to stay focused and learn.

Thank you,

Mrs. Smith, 7th grade

Today, as a CEO, vision means something entirely different, yet it also is still vitally connected to what people can see. The CEO knows where he is leading the organization. For him, vision is seeing beyond the horizon of the attainable into the future of the possible!

From what I have witnessed over the years, the clearest vision is also the most concise vision. Everyone inside the organization AND outside the organization can easily understand it. Wordiness and complexity in a vision statement are not helpful.

This reminds me of the Oscar-winning 1992 film by Robert Redford, *A River Runs Through It*, based on the book by Norman Maclean. The scene is Rev. Maclean's study. The reverend is sitting behind his desk in his study, and young Norman is bringing his homework to his stern Scottish Presbyterian father and teacher for grading. Young Norman presents his paper to his father, who marks it. Handing it back to Norman, the reverend responds, "Half as long." Norman sighs, leaves for a bit, and then returns with his rewrite. His father studies the revisions. "Again, half as long," he says, handing back the paper. Norman sighs again, leaves, and shortly after returns, handing over his work. His father takes the paper and studies it . . . looking up, he says, "Good, now throw it away." Crumpling the paper and tossing it in the trash, young Norman and his little brother Paul grab their fly-fishing gear and run toward the river.

Rapidly growing nonprofits have a vision that values the thrift in language. For them, the vision statement has been carefully crafted and pared down to its most essential wording. Even Reverend Maclean would approve!

In addition to a concise statement of vision, it also feels as though the CEO is the embodiment of the vision statement. You can see the CEO's commitment to the vision in her eyes. It is in her bearing and attitude, and you can hear it in her voice. I like to think of this as an obsession of the heart.

Trustees are in full support of the vision; in fact, they are intensely in support of it! The CEO works with the trustees as trusted friends who have invested themselves in together changing the world. Saying "they are supportive or in total alignment" is simply not adequate for rapidly growing nonprofits. The highest levels of leadership are totally sold out to the vision! They know they are part of a game-changing team.

At the risk of using too many movie metaphors, I believe it's worth sharing some insights from the 2011 film *Moneyball*. I highly recommend it to anyone who is considering embarking upon the fulfillment of a vision that challenges conventional thinking. Actually, I think I would recommend it to any leader. You don't have to be a baseball fan or even a sports fan to appreciate the many leadership lessons one can learn from this inspiring film.

It's the true story of the 2002 Oakland A's general manager, Billy Beane (Brad Pitt), who is tired of losing championship games to the "rich" teams that are forever hiring away his best players. He comes to realize that his meagerly resourced Oakland A's can't beat a team like the well-heeled New York Yankees by using traditional baseball strategies. His vision is to compete by removing money, or more specifically, the high price of talent, from the equation for winning the World Series.

His vision comes into focus only after meeting a young Yale economics graduate, Peter Brand (Jonah Hill), who follows the writings of a baseball outsider named Bill James. Billy Beane is intrigued by the statistical approach Brand employs using Bill James' scientific approach in evaluating players. Together, they develop a player recruitment strategy that has never been attempted in tradition-rich baseball. Every statistic of every member of the team is scrutinized in order to capitalize on their strengths and minimize their weaknesses to get the most runners on base, moving them from one base to another, resulting in the greatest number of runs. Together, Beane and Brand put together a no-name team that appalls all of baseball, including all the A's scouts, management, players, and especially the highly traditional and therefore obstructionist manager, Art Howe (Philip Seymour Hoffman).

No one in baseball believes in this untried, highly experimental approach. The heavy losses, early in the season, take their toll on everyone, even the faith of Beane and Brand. But Beane knows one thing for certain: he can't go back. To do so would just continue the tradition of poorer teams losing to teams with the largest payrolls.

There's a poignant moment when Beane and Brand are sitting together in Beane's office. The A's have just lost their 18th game of the season while trying to implement their new philosophy. Everyone, including the press, is calling for Billy Beane's head. The conversation comes down to this:

> **Beane:** "Do you believe in this thing or not?"
>
> **Brand:** "I do."
>
> **Beane:** "It's a problem, you think we need to explain ourselves. Don't! To anyone!"

Brand: "Okay."

Beane: "Now I'm going to see this through
for better or worse."

I'm not going to spoil the movie for you, but let's fast-forward to a comment made by John Henry, the owner of the Boston Red Sox, to Billy Beane:

"I know you're taking it in the teeth right now, but the first guy through the wall, he always gets bloody."

Having a clear vision, especially a game-changing vision, most often brings an inspired leader to a place where he "gets bloody." Inspired leaders of rapidly growing nonprofits know the truth of this intensely personal proving ground. They know the inertia of tradition has battered the vision out of many who have attempted to accomplish something out of the ordinary. Because the inspired leader is human, he has his moments of self-doubt, but he always comes back to his vision. It propels him forward against all opposition.

Her followers can see much of the strain this breaking "through the wall" places on their leader. For them, it only serves to endear her to them even more and to the vision they all share. In rapidly growing organizations, followers find themselves rallying behind this risk-taking leader, forming a phalanx that seeks to protect their leader, and the vision continues to move them forward with even greater commitment and passion.

NOTES:

NOTES:

ESSENTIAL #3
A MISSION DONORS CAN RELATE TO AND SUPPORT

Rapidly growing nonprofits have a mission that is easily stated and can be remembered . . . by everyone! The mission statement answers the question, "How can we accomplish the vision (again, *the possible vs. the attainable*)?"

The mission for a rapidly growing organization is at the core of people's beliefs and interests. In other words, the mission taps into strongly held values about something that is vital to the lives of people in the community, region, country, or world. To be effective, *it has to be easily understood and speak to the interests of all who are helping to accomplish it*, whether they are on the board, serving on the staff, volunteering, or giving the funds to bring the mission to fulfillment. It easily answers the question, "What do you do?"

Some time ago, an organization called and asked me for help with their fundraising. As I spoke to the caller, I began by asking this most basic question, "What do you folks do?" There was a pause in the conversation as the caller readied herself to give me her response. After about 10 minutes of listening, I said, "So, if I'm understanding correctly, your organization exists to help Ivy League university students, who may someday become world leaders, obtain a Christian perspective?" Again, a bit of a pause. "Yes," she said, "but we don't actually interact with the students themselves." "Hmmm," I muttered. "So who interacts directly with the students, if you don't?" "Well, actually, it's other students on Ivy League campuses who expose their classmates to Christianity." I shifted in my chair and asked another question, "So, can you be *very specific* about what your organization actually *does* to enable Christian students to share their belief system with their classmates?" She responded, a little defensively now, "It's actually quite complex. We provide literature, or to be more accurate, we write articles so Christian students can read them and formulate their own articles to be placed in Ivy League periodicals." I was getting a little dizzy now. I began looking at the time and realized that I had been on the phone for almost an hour now and wasn't getting any closer to understanding what this nonprofit did that a donor would want to support. I think you'll understand why I thanked her for calling and explained that, as a direct response fundraising agency, we couldn't provide them with effective counsel. I suggested that they contact someone who could help them formulate a case for support and then approach carefully selected foundations and high-worth individuals who could catch their vision and mission.

Many nonprofits are founded with the best of intentions. They just haven't made their vision and mission accessible or understandable to potential donors. I receive many calls from organizations who find themselves in this position. My heart aches for them as I listen to them pour their hearts out to me. I do my best to offer them what I can: a referral to someone who can coach them, free books that I have read or written that may be of help. The last thing I want to do is simply say, "Go in peace; keep warm and well fed" (James 2:16, NIV).

Lastly, the mission MUST be *believable*! Everyone involved in carrying out the mission, from trustee to donor, cannot have any lingering doubt as to the feasibility of accomplishing the mission. One of the most significant disconnects, I have witnessed, is when the mission of an organization doesn't pass the reality test. For example: "Our mission is to end poverty in the world by 2050." Now, I don't think I've ever been accused of being hard-hearted, but this just doesn't seem possible. Even Jesus said, "The poor you will always have with you, but you will not always have me" (Matthew 26:11, NIV). I realize the context of this verse and that it is not intended to be Jesus' full body of teaching about the poor. But even a person who does not spend much time reading the Bible will find it very difficult to believe this mission statement: "Our mission is to end poverty in the world by 2050."

Rapidly growing organizations have mission statements that may be challenging to accomplish, yet they are believable. Here's an example: "The Bible will be translated into every known language in the world by 2025." Admittedly, this is a giant task, and it begs the question, "How?" Which is the question this organization is wanting people to ask! They have a VERY BELIEVABLE answer!

This organization has broken the mold for how Bible translation was being done. What used to require one missionary couple one lifetime to translate Scripture into one language at an average cost of about $2 million can now be launched by a team of carefully equipped, highly committed local translators at an average cost of $19,500! It is very possible that every known language in the entire world will have the Bible within the next six years!

I'm writing this in 2019, so if you are reading this anytime after 2025, there is a very real possibility that this mission has already been accomplished. At the time of writing, this organization is already working on what's next!! This is the benefit of having a mission that donors can relate to and support.

NOTES:

NOTES:

ESSENTIAL #4
FOLLOWERS WHO SUPPORT THE VISION, MISSION, AND LEADER

Until now, we have focused largely upon the qualities of an inspired leader, as well as the vision and mission in rapidly growing nonprofits. Equally as important are the qualities of those people who are being asked to *follow* this inspired leader.

Mutual trust and respect among all levels of a rapidly growing nonprofit team are critical to building and maintaining momentum. Any inspired leader will acknowledge the challenge this represents. Any follower will acknowledge the energy and daily vigilance required of them to ensure the spirit of trust and respect among their coworkers.

Daily vigilance among followers in rapidly growing organizations is evident when a culture of listening and collaboration is the norm. The word norm is important here. When listening and collaboration are the norm, it communicates to fellow followers a sense of safety in speaking up during conversations and more formal meetings. A listening culture reinforces the importance and validation of ideas, resulting in the innovative thinking that rapidly growing nonprofits use to thrive and propel them forward.

For followers, safety and a sense of well-being are not meant to imply that everyone has a "vote," but they should feel as though they have a "respectful say" without repercussions. What I am NOT saying here is that any follower should be able to stand in their supervisor's face and challenge them publicly. A "respectful say" often begins in private, with questions such as:

- "Would you mind if I ask a question?"
- "Is it possible to hear a little more about how

you've arrived at your position on this topic?"

- "Are you open to a different perspective?"
- "Up until now, my view has been quite different. Do you mind if I share it with you?"
- "I have an idea; do you have time to hear it?"

Respectfulness is important in earning a say. And this gate swings both ways. Both followers and inspired leaders are taking risks when they engage in this kind of dialogue. Followers, as a rule, are keenly aware that they can be fired, sacked, or canned by their supervisors, especially the "big boss." While this power exists on the part of the inspired leader, here's some good news . . . *in truth, leaders are seldom considering this option.*

In rapidly growing organizations, inspired leaders know that followers are essentially *volunteers*. The leader knows and understands that followers are really *paid volunteers.* They are volunteers in that they could find meaningful employment elsewhere. They are also followers precisely because they believe in the organization and its leadership. An inspired leader doesn't take this loyalty for granted. He knows that he owes his followers the dignity of listening to them.

Just as the follower has the right to a *respectful say*, the inspired leader has the obligation to provide the follower with a *respectful listen*.

I was first introduced to the concept of respectful listening or *active listening* while attending The Institute for Charitable Giving. For many years at "The Institute," I have had the privilege of attending and experiencing the teachings of one of the master craftsmen of philanthropic solicitation, the late Bill Sturtevant. I remember the first time I participated in the institute I was thoroughly entranced and overwhelmed by the sheer volume of content pouring out of the mouth of this masterful major gifts fundraiser. His staccato delivery style made note-taking very challenging. I wanted to capture every single word Bill spoke! So, I took 40 pages of hastily written notes. It was so valuable to me, I decided to take the same course, "Seize the Opportunity," the next year, when I was able to capture another 24 pages of the golden truths being delivered in Bill's machine-gun style. It wasn't until my THIRD time taking this course that I found out Bill had a book! You'll be doing yourself a huge favor (and saving an enormous amount of money and time) by buying *The Artful Journey: Cultivating and Soliciting the Major Gift* by William T. Sturtevant. It's not a substitute for attending The Institute for Charitable Giving, mind you, but it will relieve you from the angst of trying to take verbatim notes!

I tell you all of this to emphasize this critical point: *listening is a skill that can be learned and taught*! I've listed below a few of the benefits of respectful or active listening that I learned from Bill. It begins with listening and then asking meaningful questions:

- Questions reveal needs
- Questions expose problems

- Questions reveal values
- Questions reveal motivational triggers
- Questions reveal strategic information

Inspired leaders want to glean this valuable information from their followers. Since we are focusing on followers here, it is essential for followers to hear that what they think really matters! It feels great for followers to know that they really have been listened to, and heard, by the inspired leader. By listening to them, the inspired leader is helping to build their self-confidence and creating an environment of trust and creativity.

Followers, too, have the ability to inspire self-confidence in their leaders by offering encouraging words in season. A personal example of this occurred for me a few years ago. It came when a woman from our digital team scheduled an appointment to see me one afternoon. She has been with my company well over a decade and has advanced significantly during this time. She came into my office with a gentle smile on her face. I invited her to sit and tell me what she had on her mind. What she said has been forever etched into my soul . . .

"I'm here to tell you something you may not know. I have thought about it for a long time and feel it is something I should share with you," she said.

"I hope it's good," I replied, and then we both laughed a little nervously.

"Oh, don't worry," she said. "It's good . . . I just want you to know you have changed my life by allowing me to work and advance here," she began. "What you may not know is you have also impacted my entire family. My children have a mother who is a Latina, who is not only employed in very meaningful work, but they are watching me advance in my responsibilities through your company. They have witnessed their mother realize her dreams, and now they know that they, too, can realize their own dreams!"

We sat there together, our eyes brimming with tears. After she thanked me for seeing her, she stood and quietly opened my office door and left. I was so stunned! My mind was filled with images of her husband and children feeling encouraged simply because this incredible person and employee was being treated with respect. What a gift she had just given me! Through my tears, I heard myself say, "It's working!" Clapping my hands together, I said it again, "It's really working!" You may wonder what I meant here. I think my answer is best expressed in our "Corporate Values," which were drawn up soon after our company began nearly 30 years ago:

WE VALUE:

- Long-term, mutually beneficial relationships with our clients and coworkers

- Servant leadership and an attitude of service among all staff
- Striving for excellence, both individually and as a team
- Honesty, integrity, and respect in all our dealings with clients and coworkers
- Innovation and teamwork, as a means to provide excellent service and continued growth
- Profitability, as an indicator of good stewardship and a means to sustain our business
- Diversity among our clients and staff
- Fun, humor, and a joyful work environment

As a leader, there are times for pondering the impact of your corporate values. Over the years, there have been times, such as described above, where an employee will take the time to think about what I might need to hear. It is ALWAYS a welcome and meaningful experience.

Now, let's take another view of follower behavior. Even rapidly growing organizations may have people who are not exhibiting behaviors of respectfulness, listening, and collaboration. The crucial question here is, "What does a team do when a colleague's behavior doesn't support the values and culture of their organization?" The inspired leader, upon becoming aware of the problem, knows the followers are going to address breaches of trust. He knows this is a test of the nonprofit's values. Left unaddressed, unhealthy undercurrents can begin to influence followers, thereby distracting them from being totally focused on the accomplishment of the mission. At times such as this in rapidly growing organizations, followers have the authority to address behavior, provide corrective action guidance, and ensure compliance.

If after caring guidance compliance isn't forthcoming, a process of dismissal must be undertaken. Too many organizations allow unacceptable behavior to continue unaddressed for a multitude of reasons . . . none of which are really reasonable. Followers in rapidly growing organizations understand the need to have all members of the team pulling in the same direction.

As a leader, this is a time of great testing. For a leader I'll call Tom, it came in the 15th year of his company's existence. A very senior level member of his team was undermining the values of his company with her verbally abusive behavior toward nearly everyone in the company but Tom. She was a highly intelligent person. The company's customers loved her and frequently expressed their respect for her. She was someone Tom could count on to get things done. In fact, whenever there was a project that had jumped the tracks and things were in danger of derailing the entire train, this leader would wade right in and work well into the night to put things right. At the time, Tom didn't know how their company had made it before this person had joined the team. You could say she was Tom's right arm. She was a frequent speaker at conferences, and a publisher of articles that were very well-received within the marketplace.

When Tom first began to hear rumblings of how this leader was mistreating other members of his team, he didn't believe them. But things began to really deteriorate when this key person began to undermine and verbally attack other senior members of Tom's leadership. This created a high level of dissonance within the company. When Tom began to inquire as to the nature and depth of this behavior, he didn't want to believe it.

There's a very serious and perilous aspect to behavior of this kind. This person's hostility was never directed at Tom or in his presence, so he didn't witness it firsthand. No one formally approached him with this problem. There were inferences and passing comments, but no one came to Tom with a formal request for corrective action.

It was only after bringing in a trusted leadership consultant that Tom was made fully aware of the damage being caused by this highly productive leader. His consultant said some words Tom never forgot.

They were so jarring, and yet important to the health of his company, that I believe you may find them as disturbing and helpful as Tom did. Here's what the leadership consultant said: "You have a toxic person in your leadership, and you need to do something about it. She's undermining you, not living up to your company's values, and there's another more serious problem." Tom's heart sank. "What could be more serious than this?" he asked, fearing the consultant's response. Looking Tom in the eyes, the consultant said, "Tom, by not dealing with this person, you are tacitly approving her behavior. Your employees think you are not living up to your own values! They think you approve of what she is doing because you haven't done anything to stop it!"

Tom was personally devastated! He replied, "But she is so productive." Then he said something that, at first, Tom found cavalier: "I would release a highly toxic *producer* as quickly as I would a highly toxic *nonproducer*." Tom was in agony.

There's another nuance to this story. This toxic leader had convinced Tom, and many others in the company, that only SHE could solve the big problems of their customers. Without her, the company would flounder. For years, she had set the very definition of service for Tom's firm, and in her mind, no one else measured up!

Tom's eyes had now been opened. He had to take appropriate action immediately. But it had to be done carefully and with great prudence. This leader had many followers reporting to her who also believed her to be the best thinker in the company. Anytime some difficult problem arose in serving the company's customers, these people would turn to her. "We were a 'house divided,'" Tom said. "Whatever I did next was going to be a critical test of my leadership."

Just prior to the weekend, Tom met with his toxic leader in her office. He chose his words very carefully. Here's what he said: "I really value you and all that you do for our company. For years, you have been extremely productive. There is something I need you to do now. I need for you to consider stepping out of your leadership role in your department. For years, you've indicated that you would prefer to spend more time behind the scenes. Yet I have asked you to take on direct management of our customer-facing team. You never asked for this position. I asked you to take it on, and you did exactly as I've asked. In fact, time and again I've asked you to do difficult things, and you've always done them. Thank you. Now I'm asking you to take the weekend and think about what I've just asked you to do in stepping out of your current role and taking on a new behind-the-scenes assignment." She just sat there and listened intently. She didn't give any hint of her thoughts or feelings. All she said was, "Alright, I'll think about it." Tom stood up, thanked her again for considering this position change, and told her he appreciated her efforts on the company's behalf.

The next workday following the long weekend, this highly toxic producer made an appointment to see Tom.

When the time came, she entered his office wearing a very stoic face. She held a manila folder in her hand. Tom motioned for her to have a seat and offered her coffee. She declined the coffee, and then she opened her manila folder and Tom began to realize what was coming. She quietly slid an envelope containing her resignation across the table to him.

Tom's heart sank! He wasn't ready for this to occur just yet. He was hoping for more time. Tom was hoping she would make her transition to an internally focused function and then, over time, work out their issues or negotiate her severance. But it was over, just like that!

After she left Tom's office, he closed the door, put his head down on his desk, and cried. His mind was swimming. One of his key leaders and producers had just resigned. It would be a huge hole in his team. What would his customers think? What would his staff think? Who would fill this incredible gap in the company's leadership?

After composing himself, he opened his door and asked his administrative assistant to call a meeting of his leadership team for later in the day.

As the team assembled in Tom's office, he sat there quietly and then broke the news to them. He wasn't at all prepared for their response. They were jubilant! They began talking all at once, with ideas for restructuring just pouring out of them. Tom sat there in amazement as plans for elevating younger leaders took shape on the flip chart at the end of his conference table. His leadership team had just been waiting for Tom to personally recognize the problem and to act!

Since that fateful day, a whole new attitude has been established in Tom's company. The newly elevated leaders rose to the challenge in a way that would make any CEO proud. Those who were loyal to the toxic leader were amazingly resilient. They found respect, freedom, and empowerment that they had not yet experienced. Many of them have now risen to leadership positions themselves. Today, Tom's company is experiencing a sense of trust and collaboration within that is benefiting his customers and coworkers as never before. Tom's employees are experiencing growth and joy in their work as they all pull in the same direction, sharing values and fulfilling the company's vision and mission.

As a footnote to this story, it didn't take long for all involved to realize they were being held hostage by one highly toxic leader. The company also learned that there were many better ways to serve their customers, and sales have never been better!

As followers witness the commitment of leadership to the values of their organization, it strengthens their own resolve to listen, collaborate, and focus on their own contributions.

Opportunities for personal and professional growth abound in rapidly growing nonprofits. It only follows that as the organization grows, more levels of leadership are needed. Continued growth depends upon staffing the right positions with the right people, and doing so in rapid succession.

Just as a salesman needs a "pipeline" of new sales leads, human resource departments of rapidly growing nonprofits have a pipeline of talent ready and waiting in the wings. Opportunities for existing followers to advance are plentiful because they are known entities, they already know the organization and are committed to its vision, mission, and leadership.

Each time a coworker is promoted, it is an opportunity for celebration as well as self-examination. Followers find themselves asking, "What will it take for me to be elevated in responsibility and role?" This is a key opportunity for leaders to define reality for their followers. Performance reviews provide a formal opportunity for this kind of communication, but perhaps more important are the day-to-day opportunities for definition, encouragement, and even course correction.

As a side note, when exceptional people are identified outside the organization and cash flow allows, rapidly growing nonprofits hire talented people when they become available. Whether a position is currently open or not isn't the deciding factor. The rapidly growing nonprofit knows it will need more exceptionally talented people at some point in the very near future.

Just as followers observe promotions, they are also acutely aware of when course correction has been delivered to a follower or leader. I have witnessed the development of a critical connection between followers and leaders when those leaders who require course correction in their own performance accept such feedback with grace and humility. Followers observe how leaders receive feedback from their supervisors, peers, and followers, and they emulate it! The following is a true story to illustrate this point:

There were two highly placed leaders who worked in an organization I had the privilege to serve for many years. Both leaders contributed significantly to the growth of the organization, and they rose in responsibility accordingly.

Each had their own distinct experience and leadership style. But what stood out most between them was how each handled feedback from the CEO, especially when corrective action was needed.

One of the leaders, whom I'll call Linda, at first saw the members of her team as being there to "make her look good." She drove her followers hard, was sparse with praise, and seldom recommended any of them for promotion. As with most big issues, this one came to the attention of the CEO. He did his homework and then called Linda into his office to address the grievances of Linda's team.

Linda's first response was quite defensive. She didn't deny the behaviors attributed to her; she argued that her actions and attitude toward her assigned team were appropriate. The CEO listened carefully but then leaned over his conference table, and, looking at Linda, he asked, "Is this how I have treated you over the years?" He asked his question with intensity in his voice and piercing eyes fixed directly on hers. "Well . . . no, no, I guess not," Linda responded as she looked down at the table. The CEO decided to let the awkward quiet do its work. He just sat there, observing. Linda was clearly uncomfortable in the silence that seemed to go on interminably.

Finally, she lifted her head and eyes to meet those of the CEO. "So, I obviously need to make a change in how I perceive those who report to me?" she said as a realization more than a question. They talked for several more minutes. The CEO affirmed Linda in her role but indicated there was a need for them to get together once a week for the next month or two to work through how she viewed leadership and followership.

On another occasion, the CEO found himself in a meeting with the other leader, Troy. Similar issues had surfaced, and a similar conversation commenced. But something was quite different in this meeting. While both leaders had been defensive, Troy's response was quite different from Linda's. He denied the allegations of the mistreatment of his team. He was quick to point out the weaknesses of some of his followers. When the CEO confronted him, Troy became very angry. The CEO shared some observations with Troy, both about how followers prefer to be treated and how leaders can inspire rather than punish or intimidate. With each observation, Troy defended himself. "Yes, I know this. I learned this years ago." During follow-up meetings with Troy, the CEO continued to encounter an attitude of defensiveness and anger and often heard the phrase, "Yes, I know that." It doesn't require a high level of insight to understand how Linda was able to surpass Troy in her continued growth in her career and eventually become a trusted, senior-level leader of the organization where both she and Troy served. I don't remember what happened to Troy. All I know is, I didn't hear much more about him.

Rapidly growing nonprofits are vigilant and address personnel issues quickly and head-on. Leaders and followers are in close alignment in order to accomplish the organization's mission. Problems between people simply cannot be allowed to fester.

Followers prosper when they know that any problems that arise between coworkers will be swiftly and justly resolved. Granted, just as personalities and work styles vary, followers' interpretations of "swiftly and justly" carry different expectations as well. What I've witnessed is that corporate cultures are patient in direct proportion to the level of trust that has been built through truth-telling, open communication, and reasonable time frames for action. The forward momentum of rapidly growing nonprofits is dependent upon the sense of well-being emanating from knowing "everything will be all right."

Forward momentum creates a feeling of being a part of something special. This magnetic attraction of inspired leadership and hopeful followers assists greatly in staff energy and retention. Great things are accomplished when followers are fully engaged in support of the vision.

Followers in rapidly growing organizations KNOW without a doubt that they are helping to change the world! For most of them, this is why they came to work for their employer. There are many other places where they could have invested their lives, perhaps for higher income, but they chose to be part of something special.

The continual sharing of impact stories solidifies the sense of belonging. Being able to interact directly with people who have had their lives changed by their organization becomes one of the highlights of a follower's work experience. These and other shared successes create a spirit of celebration that makes even some of the most mundane tasks bearable, especially if followers can see how these tasks add to the bigger picture of making a difference in the world.

NOTES:

ESSENTIAL #5
RESOURCES THAT CAN BE ALLOCATED FOR GROWTH

Rapidly growing nonprofits have adequate cash flow that can be allocated or reallocated to increase both program and fund development functions. For our purposes here, we will focus primarily on the latter of these two aspects of growth.

Inspired leadership has a perspective on cash reserves that allows them to translate dollars into impact. When they look at their endowment, for example, they ask the question, "What can be accomplished if we reallocate some of this capital into increasing our number of donors?" They understand that investment in acquiring new donors will be creating an ever-increasing, diversified cash base.

They also know that large donors come from people who initially give smaller donations. A person who gives an initial gift of $100 is seen as someone who is "kicking the tires" of an organization to see how they will respond. The donor is sending a message: "If you thank me promptly and tell me what my giving has accomplished, I will trust you with even more of my resources."

Of course, not all nonprofits have endowments. I can imagine someone reading this and saying, "I wish we had an endowment to use in this manner." *The good news is, you don't have to have an endowment to be able to invest in growing your donor base.* Almost every organization is the recipient of bequests. At some point, most organizations I've served over the past 35 years have received an unexpected and sizable bequest. Many have been in the seven-figure range. Even more common are bequests of $10,000-$250,000. These are often received on several occasions in any given year.

The board can approve a policy that all non-designated bequests can be used for donor acquisition for a year. They can monitor the results of this decision and decide to extend the policy for another year. Perhaps, over time, there will be enough income from newly acquired donors to provide funding for most or all of the nonprofit's donor acquisition going forward, and bequests can once again be used in other areas.

Another source of funding for donor acquisition is what many refer to as "seed funding." It can come from a major donor who is well-established in their giving of six-figure gifts. This friend of your organization, if approached with enough of the right kind of information, will very likely want to see your organization flourish. This special friend of the nonprofit can provide a special "seed gift" over and above their regular giving to be designated for the acquisition of new donors.

We served an organization that did this very thing! This historic organization did not have a budget allocated for donor acquisition, but that didn't stop their development team from looking for alternate ways to find funding for growth.

They identified a very trusted, long-term major donor who liked to think outside the box. When presented with their proposal, he committed $50,000 to use in the acquiring of new donors. Once donor acquisition opportunities were presented to specially selected prospects, the response was overwhelming! These inspiring results were shared with this same friend of the organization, and he decided to increase his giving to $100,000 for the next donor acquisition effort! Again, incredible response! Potential donors loved the offer that was presented to them through direct mail. The trusted donor shared in the excitement of growing the organization. He had caught the vision for expanding the impact of the organization through growing the donor base.

Sometimes, rapidly growing nonprofits rewrite the traditional ways of growth. Such was the case with a well-known organization involved in accelerating Bible translation.

This organization hired our company to help them speed the process of growth both with existing donors and in acquiring new donors. They had a good-sized donor file, one that many organizations would love to have. But it wasn't large enough to support the vision of their inspired leader or his leadership team. So, they decided to allocate six figures of their budget to acquiring new donors. Since this was uncharted territory for the organization, they decided to place the donor acquisition budget in a revolving fund, the idea being that once the fund was spent and replenished through the giving of these newly acquired donors, it could be used to acquire even more donors.

We struggled a bit in the beginning. It was difficult to make something as intangible as *accelerating Bible translation* into something tangible that potential donors would give to. So, we tested "offers" (specific tangible projects) to determine what potential donors would be willing to give to at an acceptable level. We found that testing concepts online was the cheapest and fastest way to determine the popular concepts.

What we learned not only surprised us, it astounded us! Effective offers most often involve asking for gifts in the $30-$50 range, but not so for this rapidly growing organization. Existing donors had already latched onto $900,000 for a new Kodiak airplane, designed by missionaries for missionaries, to carry large quantities of supplies into remote areas of the world where much of Bible translation was taking place at the time.

Our online testing of the best offers was then translated into direct mail packages that were also tested with specially selected rented mailing lists. The results of our initial direct mail testing were encouraging, so we decided to test larger segments of rented lists. We were overjoyed at the responses we were seeing from people who had never given to this organization before.

Soon, we were surprised yet again. Several potential donors decided to give $100,000! Some gave $150,000! But the real wonder came the day a potential donor sent a check for $900,000, the cost of an entire Kodiak airplane! It was not a surprise when this highly regarded organization decided to abandon the revolving fund approach and began utilizing large-scale direct mail donor acquisition year-round!

Now, I don't tell this story so you'll think we can generate major gifts for your organization through direct response donor acquisition. *I'm sharing this to impress upon you the wisdom of allocating funds for growth.* This is what rapidly growing nonprofits do!

NOTES:

ESSENTIAL #6
THE *WILL* TO EMPLOY THOSE RESOURCES

I have left this essential characteristic of rapidly growing nonprofits until last because it is the very lynchpin of growth. *Without the complete and utter commitment to fundraising growth on the part of your trustees, CEO, and leadership and development teams, rapid growth will not occur. EVERYONE* must be on board to exert his or her will to make fundraising growth occur.

As I have shown in #5 *Resources That Can Be Allocated for Growth*, a nonprofit's commitment to fundraising growth comes largely through aggressive donor acquisition. It's one of the great things about being a nonprofit; you can solicit donations! I'll state it once again: *allocating resources to donor acquisition builds into the organization's ability to grow*

EXPONENTIALLY by expanding their donor base.

It is most often the inspired leader who makes this "will to grow" possible. He understands and believes that donor acquisition is the key to growth. Once this occurs, he usually meets privately with the board chair, and then later with members of the development committee of the board (if he has one). If this group supports the concept of donor acquisition to achieve growth, it has been my experience that broader board support will follow. I'm not suggesting that unanimous support will occur at the board level. There is almost always some dissent. At the board level, it's the board chair's responsibility to move this through to a positive vote.

I remember one such board meeting where I had the privilege to attend and present a large budget for increasing a nonprofit's donor acquisition efforts. The CEO and vice president of development had very clear goals for the outcome of this meeting. They had taken the time to prepare the board development committee for the topic at hand, and the board chairman was fully briefed and in agreement with what I was being asked to present.

The meeting was held during the lunch hour, and a buffet lunch had been prepared for the members. The chairman had arrived early and provided me with insights into the group dynamics of the board. I was forewarned by the board chairman that there would be some opposition, especially from one board member in particular. He was described as being VERY fiscally conservative, and I should NOT expect him to appear pleased with ANY expenditure of money. The chairman encouraged me to not be put off or discouraged by this. He further indicated that he himself would guide the discussion.

As the board members arrived, it was evident that most of them knew each other quite well and were at ease as they circulated amongst the group, forming a line to fill their plates. I had been asked to join them for the lunch portion, and then the chairman would introduce me and I would have precisely 20 minutes to present, with another 10 minutes allocated for questions. Once my portion of the meeting was completed, I was expected to make a speedy departure in order to maximize the time for the board to discuss and make decisions.

Because it was a large board, numbering about 24 members, I had brought a colleague along to manage my PowerPoint presentation so I could focus on the board's response.

As foreseen, the prickly board member began shifting in his chair, and once the Q&A began, he came out shooting. As promised, the chairman maintained control of the meeting, allocating time for Mr. Prickly while allowing for several other members to speak as well.

It was a great example of a well-run board meeting. The CEO was in attendance, but he did not attempt to direct the meeting or respond to any board member questions or comments. He participated only as directed by the chairman. It was also very clear that the board chairman had the CEO's back.

I marveled at the ability of the chairman to convene such a well-prepared and properly conducted meeting of very accomplished people from the community who had been carefully selected to sit on this board.

It was interesting for me to watch the dynamic of the members. Each one seemed to be aware that they were part of a prestigious team. It was known throughout this great city that to be invited to serve on this board was a compliment. Even Mr. Prickly seemed to know that his opinion was in the minority and chose not to try to usurp the authority of the chairman.

The board member questions ran longer than the allotted 10 minutes, but only because the chairman knew it was time well spent and that the issue at hand deserved the time expended. Finally, noting the time, the chairman excused me and my colleague so the board could deliberate in private. I was later informed that the motion to expand donor acquisition had been passed! This organization was on its way to unprecedented growth!

As in the meeting I've just described, every step of the way, the outcome of successful donor acquisition was tied closely to the fulfillment of the vision of the organization.

Rapidly growing nonprofits have an absolute passion for the greater impact of programs resulting from growth. They will do *anything* within their means to make this happen. <u>But they also know that if they take, say, $1 million in cash reserves and spend it on programs, they'll never be exponential in their growth.</u>

They have learned that by taking the same $1 million and investing it in the acquisition of new donors, they will be replacing donors who are lapsing in their giving (this is usually about 30 percent of their donors every year). In addition, they will be expanding their donor base, thereby creating the ability to generate millions of dollars for future programs.

This is one of the most critical strategies employed by rapidly growing nonprofits! They have learned to invest a significant part of their cash reserves in preserving and growing their donor bases. When using sound direct response principles, they can expect to break even on their expenditures within a few months and increase their capacity to grow their programs, knowing they'll be able to fund them without depleting their remaining cash reserves.

As you read this, you may be asking yourself, "Isn't this a big risk? How do I know we'll get our invested funds back and see our donor base and income grow?" There's a simple answer here . . . yes, it's risky and no, you don't know if you'll receive a solid return on your investment . . . *unless you partner with someone who has a <u>proven</u> track record of success.* It's quite prudent to ask to see the results other nonprofits have realized through the efforts of the agency you're considering. An ethical agency will not reveal the names of the example organizations without their permission. But they certainly can and should produce the results of their work for others, as well as a list of references.

Donor acquisition is the most difficult aspect of direct response fundraising. It's very seldom, if ever, that a nonprofit can find and hire a fully qualified staff member who knows the cutting-edge strategies necessary to ensure success in this highly volatile/ profitable venture. Rapidly growing nonprofits know this truth.

They know that it requires a highly qualified team of strategists, writers, designers, and data analytics personnel, as well as proven digital and broadcast donor acquisition specialists. There are also subject matter experts in list selection and merge/purge functions who use highly sophisticated software.

This is why I still have a job and a company! Over the past 25 years, I have assembled a team of the most highly experienced specialists who know how to acquire donors through the mail, online, at special events, and on radio and television. They have tested everything that wiggles! They can distinguish an "offer" worth testing from a dud in a matter of seconds. Perhaps most importantly, they know what they know and what they don't know! One of the most important things they've become highly skilled at is knowing what questions to ask.

Now, I'd be both arrogant and foolish to suggest that Douglas Shaw & Associates is the only direct response fundraising agency that knows how to conduct effective donor acquisition. But I can and will say that I would put our team's capabilities up against any agency out there!

Rapidly growing nonprofits know they don't have to go it alone. They also know there is no wisdom in trying to shortchange the process necessary to achieve success in donor acquisition by trying to do it themselves. For example, for eight years, I had the privilege of serving a nonprofit aiding blind people. During this time, I learned *so much* about blindness, but also about many of the ancillary issues surrounding those who are without sight. I distinctly remember the comments of a woman in her

30s sitting on the veranda of a lodge at a camp for the blind in downstate New York. I was interviewing her for an income-producing newsletter I had created for the organization. She said, with tears in her eyes, "All I'm looking for is the opportunity to show someone that I'm worthy of a job. I'm blind . . . not stupid!" Until that very moment, I had not even considered how it must feel to have to live with false assumptions being made about me every single day of my life.

False assumptions can be very harmful to individuals; they hurt them and beat them down. These assumptions can also do great harm to nonprofits seeking rapid growth. Yet, in my experience, many organizations make many false assumptions about themselves! One of the biggest of these assumptions is when a nonprofit decides to attempt doing donor acquisition in-house in order to save money.

This is exactly what this organization serving the blind decided to do. I had helped them through many years of donor acquisition. We had developed sound strategies, including strong offers and high-performing direct mail packages (digital acquisition had not yet come into its own at this time). We had selected and carefully tested mailing lists that would perform well, resulting in an escalating growth of the nonprofit. But all of this was lost when they decided to attempt this most difficult of fundraising exercises without the perspective of experienced counsel.

The first false assumption they made was to believe they could save more money on donor acquisition by simply "exchanging" lists with other organizations serving the blind and thereby avoid the costs of renting responsive mailing lists. This decision alone caused them great harm. They offered up their loyal donors to other causes serving blind people in exchange for the names of less effective lapsed donors, and soon many of their best donors began receiving direct mail appeals from many more causes serving the blind. Some of their best donors asked to be removed from their mailing list;

others transferred their loyalty to other organizations that were also serving blind people.

There were many other well-intentioned assumptions made that lowered response rates and decreased average gift sizes. *But the biggest false assumption they made was to believe they could generate the same number of donors giving the same average gifts by spending less money.* I only know this because they called me back two years later to help them repair the damage.

Rapidly growing nonprofits challenge their own assumptions. Instead of making assumptions, they ask good questions like, "Who do we know who can help us grow our donor file quickly?" They use the strengths of trusted consultants when they do not have the internal expertise they need.

They also know and embrace the old adage, "You get what you pay for!" It requires the exercising of great faith and courage to stay focused on the things in which the nonprofit excels (e.g., spreading the good news, rescuing the victims of sex trafficking, or providing clean drinking water). *Rapidly growing nonprofits are growing precisely because they know what they are good at and ask for help with things outside their expertise.*

It's absolutely amazing to see all the good that can be accomplished when it is the will of a nonprofit to allocate their resources to growth! It literally changes a community, a region, a province or state, a country, and, in many cases, the world!

I have never met a leader of a nonprofit who wanted to lead a declining organization. No one I know has accepted a trustee invitation to leadership with anything but the hope of growth of the impact of his or her new assignment for service.

But I HAVE met many leaders (i.e., trustees or CEOs) who have, by their own beliefs, assumptions, and actions, stymied the growth of the organization they have committed to serve and grow. Why would they do this, you may ask? It most often has to do with leadership belief about fundraising.

Let me be the first to say, I do not believe leaders participating in this negative outcome are intending to do harm. In fact, it's my experience that most feel they are embracing historic values, being faithful to organizational tradition, or have developed a personal theology or philosophy of fundraising to which they hold deeply. Sadly, I have even seen personal preferences, fear of the unknown, and exaggerated egos in leadership prevent organizations from growth. I encounter this self-inflicted wound all too often. Unfortunately, their firm commitments run contrary to proven best practices, and it is the very people their organization seeks to help who are negatively impacted. This is exactly why I have written this book. It is intended to help you avoid the rockslides and unforeseen crevices along the upward path to the rapid growth of your nonprofit. May it serve you well.

CONCLUSION

At the outset of this journey, I offered my own list of the six essential characteristics shared by rapidly growing nonprofits. It is my deepest hope that my observations have confirmed that your organization is getting ready to take off, in full flight, or making the plans necessary to ensure the upward rise you seek.

The stories I've used to illustrate these characteristics are true, because I find real life far more interesting and inspiring than fiction. I hope that this decision I've made is an encouragement to you that all nonprofits can be readied for rapid growth, and in so doing make our world a much better place for those of us who inhabit it.

It's my belief that the positive impact of well-run nonprofit organizations is the embodiment of hope that so much of humankind seeks. As a person of faith, I believe this is what our Creator would have us do. Thank you for being part of what is right with the world!

NOTES:

ADDENDUM

While exploring some of the documents stored in the annals of our company, the following was recently rediscovered by some of our leadership. When they read it, they were surprised that it was written more than 20 years ago, and these principles are still in use in our company today. I've included it here at the request of those leaders.

THE PRINCIPLES FOR SERVICE

By Douglas K. Shaw

Chairman/CEO, Douglas Shaw & Associates, Inc.

Fundraising Counsel

In order to do what we are supposed to do, we must live by a set of principles. I believe the Bible to be the basis for any good principle worth embracing.

In order to strengthen you in your current position, and to help you as you seek to improve your skills and serve at a higher level, I believe I owe you a framework for working and for your personal improvement within our company.

I. Trust

<u>Without Clients, We Have No Business</u>

Unless a client trusts us to serve them, we don't have a reason to exist as Douglas Shaw & Associates, Incorporated. Therefore, **client trust is our highest corporate goal.** Everything else follows this: corporate and personal profitability, professional growth, and a sense of accomplishment in a job well done.

<u>Client Trust Is Earned, Not Bestowed</u>

A client decides to hire us because they need help and they think they can trust us to provide it. They don't hire us because they like us, though we desire that they do like us. They hire us because they believe we will help them with their need.

Even if a client begins with a sense of trust, we must realize that trust is fragile. It can quickly vanish if it is not properly cared for. Our client's sense of trust can build and grow with each passing day, or it can diminish and wither.

When a client signs a contract with Douglas Shaw & Associates, Inc., they are making a profession of hope. They hope that we can meet their needs. For us, this hope is a starting point for trust, but only that; a starting point.

As long as things run smoothly, this hope is not challenged or dashed. But things seldom run smoothly for very long. Mistakes are made, communication lapses, something happens to threaten our plans and the client's hope.

When our client's hope is challenged, we face an opportunity. Our first opportunity is to own up to our mistakes. We must personally and corporately "own the problem." It exists, and it's "ours."

If the mistake is "ours," then we face our second opportunity—we get to make it right. If that means absorbing some of the cost of a project, then that's exactly what we'll do. **A project is nothing compared to a relationship.** We want our client to feel they have done the right thing in placing their trust in us.

The third opportunity we face is to show our client that we learn from our mistakes. We examine ourselves, make corrections, and communicate our corrective action to our client. This demonstrates that we took our mistake seriously and will work to prevent it in the future. At this point, trust begins to grow.

I have found that trust grows more quickly when mistakes are made, owned, and corrected than when there are no mistakes.

Trust-building requires time. There is no substitute for longevity of relationship. In fact, real trust requires the passage of time. The ups and downs of life with our client strengthen our relationship.

Broken trust is more work than paying attention. In fact, broken trust can often be fatal to a client relationship. It occurs when a client reaches a place where they simply "can't trust us anymore." We must avoid this chasm with all that is in us.

We Build Trust When We Keep Promises

Simple things build trust. Things like returning phone calls on time and when promised, being prompt for meetings, and following through on commitments go a long way toward establishing trust. "If they say it, it'll happen" is some of the highest praise to which we can aspire.

When a client hires us, they are hiring us to create greater net income than they believe they can achieve on their own. Most prospective clients want us to tell them how much money we think we can raise for them. We have to use great wisdom in how we respond.

An income forecast is perceived as a promise. While no mortal can see the future, we can construct likely outcomes based upon our experience. While we may use words like "forecast" and "projection," our numbers still create expectations by boards, CEOs, and CFOs.

We can tell some clients what we believe we can raise for them. There are other clients for whom there is simply not enough information available to adequately project revenue. We must have the courage to be truthful with our prospective clients. **Courage today will build trust tomorrow.**

When we don't achieve our forecast, we face an opportunity to build trust. This is first done by sharing in our client's disappointment, acknowledging it, agreeing with it, and committing to determine the reasons for it. Defensiveness has no place in this process. Honesty must prevail. Every effort must be made to determine the cause of our failure in order to ensure more accurate forecasting in the future.

We Build Trust When We're Honest

Honesty is hard to find. I believe it's hard because we all have the same reaction that Adam and Eve had in the Garden. Our human reaction is to hide from mistakes. It's all too tempting to cover a mistake with a lie. Then the problem compounds. Then a cover-up has taken place. When the cover-up is exposed (and we need to assume it will be), trust is betrayed. **Again, courage in the short term is less frightening than admitting to lying, and less humiliating too!**

II. Competence

Competence Helps Trust Flourish

We can be honest with our clients about our mistakes, but we dare not communicate incompetence. Incompetence suggests that the client thinks we're honest but, "simply in over their heads."

Competence begins in knowing what we're doing. It means we know our business and we know it well. But it means we also understand the "why" of our business.

Knowing the "why" of our business means every employee has the opportunity to understand how his or her job is critical to our overall purpose—earning the trust of our clients.

Knowing the "why" gives us all permission to question our assumptions. If we know why we are doing something, it gives us a basis for asking good questions. Knowing the "why" makes us able to build competence.

Competence is demonstrated to clients every time we accomplish what we promise. If we say a deadline will be met, it's met. If we say a call will be returned at 4:00 p.m., it's returned at 4:00 p.m. If we say we can increase income by 20 percent over last year, then we raise 20 percent more!

Competence means we will expend every effort to keep our promises. But even more important, competence means we succeed. It means the effort was expended and the promise was indeed kept. "They said they'd get it done, and they did."

Competence is possible when we know the tools of our trade. Just like the brick mason, whose trowel fits his hand, so should our tools fit us. Trowel handles get shaped to the mason's hand only after years of continual use.

Repetition Builds Competence

The confidence-building act of repetition makes us more familiar with our tools and better at what we do.

Doing something over and over brings a special familiarity into our minds and our experience. It makes us sure. It creates confidence, which leads us to competence.

III. Caring

Caring Is a Matter of the Heart

Caring means that our heart is in our work and our work matters to us. I believe caring is something that can be "caught but not taught." Just as you can tell if someone cares about you by what they do, so it is with caring about our work. What we do reflects how we feel, and it communicates where our heart is.

Caring about our clients builds trust. If we genuinely care about their mission, their donors, and their success, they can tell, and it inspires their trust in us.

Caring about our client's work is a tangible expression of our hearts' inclination.

But caring is expensive. It costs us something. It makes us vulnerable; it makes us strong.

It's expensive because it requires that we "work until it's done right." There are no shortcuts. Even on a Friday night, it needs to be done right. In the midst of peak season, it needs to be done right.

It costs us time because it requires double- and triple-checking to make sure something's been done right.

It makes us vulnerable because none of us is perfect, so we need each other for a new set of eyes to review our

work. It requires a team effort and joint purpose. It
means we are all subject to review.

The end result makes us strong. Our work is better.
Our clients are pleased, and we are able to celebrate a job
well done.

IV. Vigilance

<u>Vigilance Leads Us to Excellence</u>

"To be alertly watchful, especially of danger" is how
Webster's Dictionary defines vigilance. It means we're
constantly on the lookout for mistakes-in-the-making
and anything that jeopardizes the competent execution
of our work.

**The sooner we detect problems, the more options
we'll have to deal with them.** This is especially true in a
production environment, where there are so many
opportunities for error.

In order to detect problems, we must first be looking
for them. We have to know what they look like and when
they usually appear. We have to know how one problem

might spawn another. We must constantly be checking our own work and the work of each member of our team.

When, through vigilance, we find a problem, we must reward the finder. When a "good catch" is made, it solves problems for us all. Ben Franklin's adage, "A stitch in time saves nine," applies nicely here. Catching a small problem keeps us from having a large problem, i.e., an unhappy client. We need to offer encouragement, recognition, and praise to anyone catching a problem in its early stages.

Thankfully, most tears can be mended, and most problems can be solved. With vigilance, we can avert most problems that can grow into crises.

But when a crisis does occur, we must handle it honestly and straight on.

V. The Gift of Focus

The Ability to Concentrate in the Midst of Clamor

There's a Yiddish saying that means literally, "stop banging the pot." It is used when someone is expressing the feeling, "stop bothering me."

With all the deadlines we face and all the priorities we set, we are bound to have conflicting timelines and interests. Our challenge is not only to be civil and caring to each other in the midst of the fray, but also to remain alert and accurate in our assessments.

Focus requires our full concentration. In order for excellence to prevail, our thinking has to be clear and our decisions and judgments must be right.

Focus also requires mutual sensitivity. If we observe our coworker trying to proofread something or trying to concentrate on a phone call, we need to move our conversation away from our coworker in order to allow them to focus more fully on the task at hand. Not all of us have doors, and therefore they can't be closed to drown out the din.

Lack of focus can also come from within. When our heads are spinning with personal issues, if we're feeling tired, ill, or just feeling the sheer weight of being overwhelmed by work, we need to give ourselves permission to clear our heads.

For me, focus comes through being able to complete one task at a time. Because we are in the service business, we make our living by being responsive. That means when the telephone rings, we answer it. When a project completes a step, we move it to the next step. When a question needs answering, we answer it. When a signature is needed, we give it. When the urgency of these things begins piling up, it's easy to lose focus.

This loss of focus causes errors in judgment. A hasty signature or a hurried client phone call often results in a problem down the line. It's important that we learn to regain our focus quickly. This can often be done through positive communication. You can ask someone if they can wait until they can have your full attention. You can ask if you can meet in 10 minutes when you've completed the task at hand. You can close your door if you have one. You can ask coworkers to take phone calls for the next hour so you can concentrate.

When we are focused as individuals and as a company, our clients are well served and their trust in us continues and grows.

VI. The Art of Asking Questions

Some people are embarrassed to ask questions. I often hear the statement given just prior to asking a question, "This may be a stupid question, but . . ."

But, for us, stupidity doesn't come in the asking of a question. If stupidity comes at all, it's more in the ignoring of someone's legitimate desire to learn.

Questions are a good thing. They are the doorways to the satisfaction of our need to know. They are also the essential building blocks of service.

We will better serve God, ourselves, our families, our colleagues, and our clients if we can bring ourselves to the point of responding to the qualifier, "This may be a stupid question" with the healing response of, "There is no such thing as a stupid question." This response is healing because it "legitimizes" the person asking the question.

Our openness to questions put to us by others creates a sense of approachability and an environment for learning. When our clients ask us questions, they are doing several things.

In the beginning of a relationship, they are often testing us. They want to know if we are knowledgeable and trustworthy. They are also seeking confirmation that their organization's decision to hire us was a good one.

Questions are a good means of testing knowledge. By asking questions, our new client is able to determine the parameters of our knowledge. "How well do they know their business?" "Can we trust their experience?" "What are the limits of their expertise?"

As our relationship with our client grows, the questions often become more task-related. These kinds of questions are often simply practical, such as, "Should I put first-class postage on all major donor communication?" Task-oriented questions are good, because they increase our client's knowledge and imply a growing sense of trust on the part of our client.

How we respond to task-oriented questions will determine how deep our relationship will grow. If we are reliable in small things, then it's likely that we'll be perceived as being reliable in large things. If we don't disparage the person asking the question or treat the question as though it was simple and respond with, "I thought everybody knew that!" then we have strengthened our relationship with our client.

We truly become partners with our clients when we can learn to ask questions together, in the spirit of learning, without condemnation or judgment. Larry Pitcher, now-retired president of Christian Record Services (CRS), was one of our longest-standing clients and is a consummate student. He can never learn enough. Several times throughout the year, we would exchange the names of books and authors who gave us new ideas for the growth of the CRS organization. Each of us respected the other's expertise, and each of us challenged the other to learn and practice our respective crafts at even higher levels. This is the ultimate in learning and trust, that we can freely ask questions together!

We owe our clients more than answers to their questions. Because of what we do, we must give away the very things that give us value—our expertise, our knowledge, and our experience. For this reason, we must give our clients more than what they should do; we must also give them the why. Giving our clients the why is tantamount to giving them the principal as well as the interest on our investments.

To give our clients the "why," we must first know it ourselves. This only comes through our own asking of questions.

My mother told the story of one of us kids growing up. All day long, the child of note followed her around the house, asking, "Why come?" this and "Why come?" that. Finally, my mother, growing weary of being followed, turned to her little pursuer, placed her hands on her hips, and said, "Why come? To you!" The little one looked surprised and said, "Why come you why come?" In spite of what you may be thinking, I have no direct evidence that this child was me.

Asking questions puts us in a position of learning. Since all we have to offer our clients is our expertise, we must always be creating and obtaining new and helpful knowledge. In order for this to occur, we must always be students of our craft.

Ken Follett, in his novel *Pillars of the Earth*, describes the life and times of the men and women who built and used the great cathedrals of Europe. The central character is the master builder, Tom, who becomes known as Tom Builder. Tom teaches his son Jack all he knows about his trade, but it's simply not enough to meet the demands of the day. His clients are requiring ever-higher walls and ceilings in their growing appetites for grand cathedrals. But with each attempt, the ceilings fall, and the walls buckle. Lives are lost, and kingdoms are put in jeopardy. Tom knows his trade well, but he has limits to his expertise. So, his son Jack, now himself a master carver of stone, sets off to Spain, hoping to get work on the new cathedrals under construction there. In Spain there were new methods, and in Spain he found his answer, flying buttresses! We must always be seeking the "flying buttresses" of our business to enhance the solid foundations we lay for our clients.

VII. The Power of Principles and the Pitfall of Assumptions

God-honoring service requires that we know and use time-tested principles for service. There is strength in coming to know principles. They are tools we can use to build both familiar and unfamiliar structures for our clients.

Principles are internalized knowledge. They are ours. We now own them. They're not someone else's experiences; they are our own.

Max DePree calls this process, "Finding our own voice." It comes when we internalize knowledge within the realm of our own experiences. We begin to find ourselves telling our own stories in our own words rather than always quoting someone else.

There is great strength and value in owning your own principles. But it must be said that there are also pitfalls that can lead to the breaking of trust with clients.

We must all make assumptions in carrying out our tasks. But we need the wisdom to identify and test our assumptions. We would do well to emulate the cockpit check process required by the FAA. If ever there is an occasion when something should not be assumed, it's when preparing to take off or land in a jet carrying 200 or more people. The pilot says, "Landing gear down!" The copilot verifies, "Landing gear down!" What can feel like tedious repetition serves us all well. If the pilot didn't put the landing gear down and the copilot assumed the pilot knew what he was doing, the results would be disastrous!

One of the ways we serve our clients well is by documenting our assumptions. This helps to establish our thought process as we develop strategies. That's one of the reasons I have my office walls papered with flip chart pages. I have to see my thought process to test it. I encourage you to use whatever process is most helpful to you. Each of us has our own preferences and style, but the principle here is to identify your assumptions and document them too.

Documenting our assumptions helps us to see them and to challenge them. It also allows those around us to think with us and point out areas of concern, uncertainty, or obvious success or error. Testing assumptions is a constructive, helpful process. It helps us to avoid pitfalls and accusations of being "all speed and no direction."

When applying the principles of our craft to a new area, it is critical that we not only document our assumptions, but also involve our clients in creating them. This allows them to own the process, as well as understand the speculative nature of a new venture. It also provides corporate memory during critical checkpoints along the way: "Now, what did we say this donor would give in May? Was it $5,000 or $50,000?"

VIII. Prioritizing Our Time

Knowing *what* to do for our clients is quite different from knowing when to do it. With all of the relationships we seek to build, maintain, and grow, we need to be both efficient and effective.

Efficiency, it has been said, is "doing things right," whereas "effectiveness is doing the right thing." Given the ever-increasing speed of life and our business, becoming "priority-sensitive" is all the more essential.

It amazes me what the digital revolution is making possible. A photo can be taken at noon in Toledo and, because of the internet, become part of a graphic design in a newsletter in Chicago by 12:01 p.m.! We all thought, "What did I do before Federal Express?" **Speed requires priority to be effective. When we move at internet speed, we must be able to choose our words and actions quickly but nonetheless carefully.** Split-second decisions require familiarity with our craft. This familiarity added to inventiveness, speed, and effectiveness all contribute to trust, and, in the end, it all comes back to **trust.**

Summary

As you grow in your thinking and in your work, you may want to develop your own personal *Principles for Service*. It's my hope that your principles might overlap, build upon, and expand some of these. I also hope you will share yours with the rest of us as we work together to build a company that builds the trust of our clients and our faith in each other.

BIBLIOGRAPHY

DePree, M. (2004). *Leadership Is an Art*. New York: Crown Publishing.

Kurson, R. (2018). *Rocket Men*. New York: Random House.

McCullough, D. (2001). *John Adams*. New York, NY: Simon & Schuster.

Miller, B. (Director). (2011). *Moneyball* [Motion Picture].

Redford, R. (Director). (1992). *A River Runs Through It* [Motion Picture].

Sturtevant, W. T. (2004). *The Artful Journey: Cultivating and Soliciting the Major Gift*. Chicago: Institutions Press.

The Holy Bible, New International Version. (1984). Colorado Springs, CO: International Bible Society.

The Institute for Charitable Giving. 500 North
Michigan Avenue, Suite 2008, Chicago, Illinois 60611,
Phone: (800) 234-7777, www.instituteforgiving.org

ABOUT THE AUTHOR

Douglas Shaw is the author of *The Rules of Fundraising* and *More Rules of Fundraising*. He is the founder of Douglas Shaw & Associates, Inc., a leading international fundraising consulting firm with offices in Chicago. He's been involved in raising funds for nonprofits for the last 42 years, raising hundreds of millions of dollars for more than 300 nonprofit organizations and ministries. He's the publisher of *Donor Focus*, a newsletter for nonprofit leaders, and a regular contributor to publications serving the nonprofit community.

He serves as Chairman of the Board/CEO of Douglas Shaw & Associates and is a sought-after speaker on fundraising and leadership. His informal, personal style appeals to audiences of all types. Doug has conducted special events with entertainment and political celebrities such as George and Barbara Bush, James and Susan Baker, Lloyd Ogilvie, Art Linkletter, and former congressman J.C. Watt. He produced nonprofit endorsement radio and television commercials with former President Ronald Reagan.

Doug's commitment to ethical fundraising has earned him a reputation as a straight shooter and effective practitioner of the rules of fundraising and servant leadership. He is married to Kathryn Shaw and has two grown children, Laura and Graham. He and his wife live in the Pacific Northwest.

DON'T MISS THESE OTHER TITLES BY DOUGLAS SHAW

THE RULES OF FUNDRAISING

The Rules of Fundraising is an authoritative guide for nonprofits. Written by Douglas K. Shaw, Founder/Chairman of the Board and CEO of Douglas Shaw & Associates, this book provides insights from years of assisting organizations around the world.

MORE RULES OF FUNDRAISING

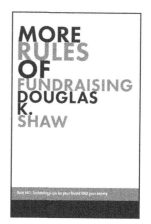

More Rules of Fundraising—a continuation of *The Rules of Fundraising*—provides more insights on fundraising that you can put into practice immediately to enhance your fundraising efforts.

REQUEST YOUR COPY TODAY!

Scan this QR code to request a **FREE** copy of these fundraising resources—and request multiple copies for your team!

DOUGLAS SHAW
& *Associates*
FUNDRAISING COUNSEL

info@douglasshaw.com
630-562-1321
www.douglasshaw.com

OTHER WAYS TO
CONNECT WITH
DOUGLAS SHAW & ASSOCIATES:

FUNDRAISING TIPS
FOR EVERY ORGANIZATION!

Scan this QR code to sign-up for
our free newsletter *Donor Focus*

ACCESS HOURS
OF FUNDRAISING
CONVERSATIONS!

Scan this QR code to
browse our free
webinar library

DOUGLAS SHAW
& Associates
FUNDRAISING COUNSEL

info@douglasshaw.com
630-562-1321
www.douglasshaw.com